William Shakespeare

Oxford University Press, 198 Madison Avenue, New York, NY 10016

Oxford New York
Athens Auckland Bangkok Bogotá Buenos Aires
Calcutta Cape Town Chennai Dar es Salaam Delhi
Florence Hong Kong Istanbul Karachi Kuala Lumpur
Madrid Melbourne Mexico City Mumbai
Nairobi Paris São Paulo Singapore
Taipei Tokyo Toronto Warsaw

and associated companies in
Berlin Ibadan

Oxford is a trademark of Oxford University Press

Text © Haydn Middleton 1997
Illustrations © Oxford University Press 1997
Published by Oxford University Press, NY, 1998
Originally published by Oxford University Press UK in 1997

Library of Congress Cataloging-in-Publication Data

Middleton, Haydn.
    William Shakespeare: the master playwright / Haydn Middleton;
illustrated by Gerry Ball.
        p.   cm.—(What's their story?)
    Includes index.
    1. Shakespeare, William, 1564–1616—Biography—Juvenile
literature.   2. Dramatists, English—Early modern, 1500–1700—
Biography—Juvenile literature.   [1. Shakespeare, William,
1564–1616.   2. Authors, English.]   I. Ball, Gerry, 1940-   ill.
II. Title.   III. Series.
PR2895.M6   1998
822.3'3—dc21
[B]   97–32049
                                                                    CIP
                                                                    AC

1 3 5 7 9 10 8 6 4 2

ISBN 0-19-521430-7 (hardback)

Printed in Dubai by Oriental Press

William Shakespeare

THE MASTER PLAYWRIGHT

HAYDN MIDDLETON

Illustrated by Gerry Ball

OXFORD UNIVERSITY PRESS

In April 1564, a baby boy was born to the Shakespeare family. They named him William, or Will for short. He would grow up to become the most famous English writer of all time.

The Shakespeares lived in Stratford-upon-Avon, a leafy little market town in the heart of England. A hundred miles to the south lay London, the capital, where Queen Elizabeth I had her court. A hundred miles was a long way in those days. Most people in Stratford knew about London only from stories. It must have sounded like a huge and dangerous place to be.

But Stratford could be dangerous, too. In the summer after Will was born, a disease called the plague killed more than 200 of the Shakespeare family's neighbors.

Luckily, baby Will survived.

Will was the eldest of six children. Their home was large and lively. Will's mother, Mary, came from a very wealthy local family. His father, John, was a glove maker and leather merchant, and he also worked for the town council. His duties included tasting the beer made in Stratford to make sure it was good.

There was a grammar school in the town, with teachers from Oxford University. The pupils there learned subjects like Latin, Greek, and religion. Parents and teachers alike harshly punished children who misbehaved.

But sometimes there were wonderful treats. Young Will's favorite was going to see one of the traveling companies of actors that sometimes came to town. The actors would set up a stage wherever there was a space and perform the latest plays.

Will loved these shows. He dreamed of joining a company one day and being an actor himself. He might even write some plays! But at 19 he was still in Stratford—with a family of his own to look after.

Anne Hathaway was a farmer's daughter. She lived in nearby Shottery, just on the edge of the Forest of Arden. Although she was eight years older than Will, they fell in love, and in 1582 they got married. During the next two years they had three children: first Susanna, and then the twins, Hamnet and Judith.

Will did whatever jobs he could find to earn money to support them all. But his thoughts were often elsewhere. Every time a band of traveling actors passed through town, Will remembered how once he had longed to be an actor and a playwright.

He loved his home and family, but he needed more from life.

Anne knew that Will felt unhappy. She also knew that if he got the right chance, he could be a good actor and writer. But if he joined a traveling company, she and the children could not travel with him. Life on the roads of England could be violent and unsafe.

So they came to an arrangement. Will would go off alone to try to make his name. But he would send back money to his family and keep coming home whenever he could.

When the next band of actors came to Stratford, Will begged them to let him join. He would do anything, even look after the horses! He seemed such an eager and lively young man that they took him on. And off he went to follow his dreams.

Will's travels had begun. They took him, in the end, to bustling London.

London was like nowhere Will had ever seen (or smelled)! Fabulously rich people lived alongside the desperately poor. Grand buildings such as the Tower of London and St. Paul's Cathedral dwarfed the filthiest slums. And through it all ran the teeming river Thames— by far the busiest highway in the city.

There were plenty of ways for Londoners to enjoy themselves. Listening to religious talks was very popular. So was watching "sports" like cockfighting and bearbaiting. But the newest thing was the open-air theater, where paid actors performed plays.

It cost very little to get into a theater. Everyone went to watch plays, from apprentice boys to elegant courtiers.

Will was a good actor, and he worked hard to make himself even better. By 1592 he was well known in the London playhouses. He was also performing in plays by a very talented new writer: himself.

Will began by writing serious plays about English kings from the past—he always loved history. But then he wrote some funny plays as well, for example, *The Comedy of Errors*. Meanwhile, he was also writing some wonderful love poems.

People soon saw that Will had true genius. Wealthy noblemen liked to boast that they knew him. The earl of Southampton became his personal patron, or sponsor, and rewarded him well for writing his poems. Companies of his fellow actors also loved his work and could not wait to get their hands on each new play he wrote.

After 1594 Will acted and wrote for just one company: the Lord Chamberlain's Men. Other members included William Kempe, London's best comic actor, and Richard Burbage, a great hero in tragedies—plays with sad plots. Will kept these actors in mind whenever he wrote a new play. He gave Burbage a marvelous leading part in one of them: *Romeo and Juliet*.

omeo and Juliet is a typically action-packed Shakespeare play. The hero and heroine are two young lovers in the Italian city of Verona. They have to keep their love a secret because their families are bitter enemies. They get married, but then there is a tragic mix-up. Romeo, thinking that Juliet is dead, kills himself with poison. When Juliet finds out, she stabs herself to death.

People watching plays in Will's time were not expected to keep quiet. So this heartbreaking love story would have given audiences plenty to cheer and boo. But they would not have seen a woman playing Juliet. Female parts were played by boys, lavishly dressed up to look feminine. Companies of actors were always on the lookout for costumes.

When rich men died, they sometimes left their clothes to their servants. The servants would then sell them to companies like Will's.

At last Will was doing what he wanted and making a success of it. But then a real-life tragedy struck.

Will was so busy that he rarely had time to return to his family in Stratford-upon-Avon, which was two days' ride away. In August 1596 he made the journey, but it was a very sad one. His son, Hamnet, just 11 years old, had fallen ill and died.

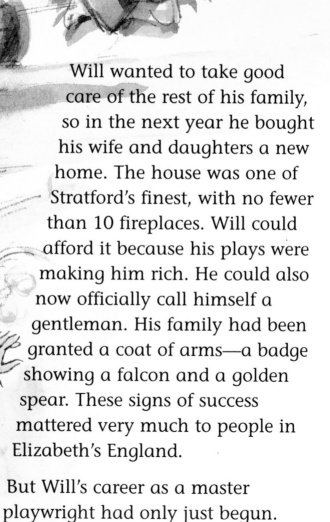

Will wanted to take good care of the rest of his family, so in the next year he bought his wife and daughters a new home. The house was one of Stratford's finest, with no fewer than 10 fireplaces. Will could afford it because his plays were making him rich. He could also now officially call himself a gentleman. His family had been granted a coat of arms—a badge showing a falcon and a golden spear. These signs of success mattered very much to people in Elizabeth's England.

But Will's career as a master playwright had only just begun.

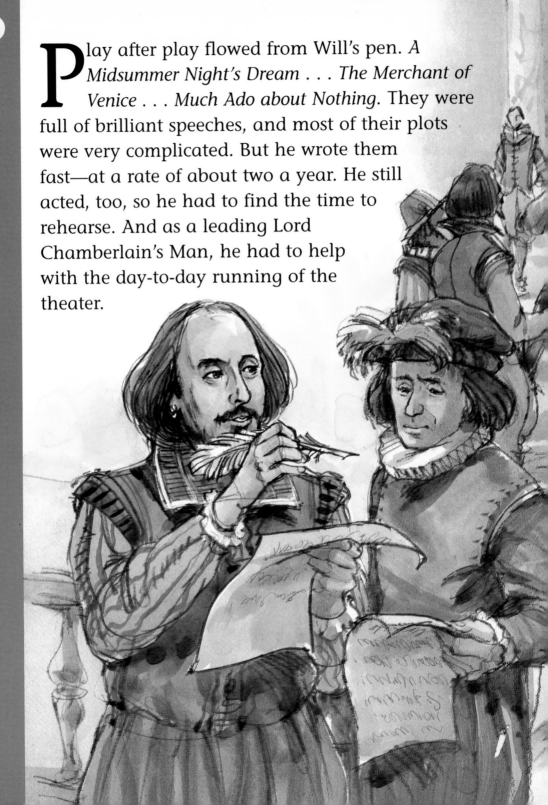

Play after play flowed from Will's pen. *A Midsummer Night's Dream . . . The Merchant of Venice . . . Much Ado about Nothing.* They were full of brilliant speeches, and most of their plots were very complicated. But he wrote them fast—at a rate of about two a year. He still acted, too, so he had to find the time to rehearse. And as a leading Lord Chamberlain's Man, he had to help with the day-to-day running of the theater.

But Will never ran out of energy— or ideas for his plays. He also put in lots of special effects for his audiences to enjoy. Cannonballs were rolled around to make the sound of thunder. Actors hid bladders full of pigs' blood under their costumes, which spurted open when they were stabbed.

Thanks to all Will's efforts, the Lord Chamberlain's Men went from one success to another. In 1599 they even built their own theater. It happened in a rather strange way.

The company had been performing at a playhouse in north London. The land that it stood on belonged to a man named Giles Allen. In 1598 Allen decided that he wanted to use the land for other purposes.

The company argued with Allen over who owned the playhouse itself. The argument went on and on. Finally, late one night, the actors and some workmen came and carefully dismantled the building. They took all the timber, put it in boats, and ferried it across the Thames. There, on the river's south bank, they built a new playhouse with it. Allen was furious. He tried to take the Lord Chamberlain's Men to court, but he failed.

The new theater was called the Globe. It quickly became a great success. Audiences of 2,500 people flocked in to watch Will's plays. One of them was the great tragedy *Hamlet*.

"To be or not to be: that is the question." So began one of the finest speeches Will ever wrote. It was spoken by a worried young man named Hamlet, the prince of Denmark, in the play named after him.

Hamlet's uncle has secretly murdered Hamlet's father and married his mother. His father's ghost then appears and tells Hamlet what has happened. Hamlet knows that he has to take revenge, but his plans go terribly wrong. One death follows another until, at the play's end, hardly anyone is left alive.

Hamlet was very popular. Soon students were performing it, too, and even some sailors on a long ocean voyage put on a show. The ship's captain was happy for his men to be acting out Will's tragedy. He said that it kept them out of mischief!

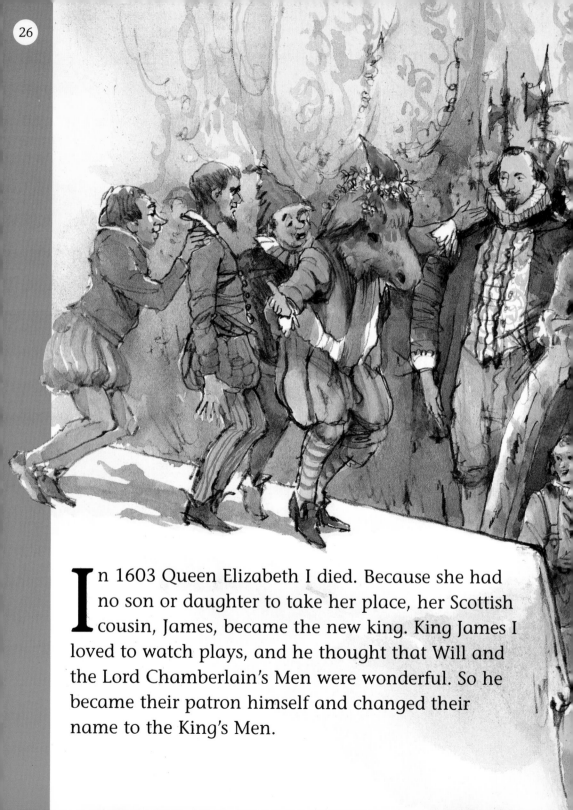

In 1603 Queen Elizabeth I died. Because she had no son or daughter to take her place, her Scottish cousin, James, became the new king. King James I loved to watch plays, and he thought that Will and the Lord Chamberlain's Men were wonderful. So he became their patron himself and changed their name to the King's Men.

During the next 10 years, the King's Men performed nearly 200 times at the royal court. Sometimes Will had to cut out pieces from his plays, in case they made the king bored, or shocked him. Meanwhile he went on writing masterpieces for all theatergoers to enjoy: *Othello, Macbeth, King Lear, Antony and Cleopatra.* Many of his later plays were dark tragedies. The wonder of his words kept audiences spellbound for hours.

Open-air theaters were used only in summer, when the weather was good. So in 1609 the King's Men took over a roofed-in theater called Blackfriars. It was smaller than the open-air Globe, and people had to pay more to watch plays there. But the King's Men could now perform by spooky candlelight on cold winter nights.

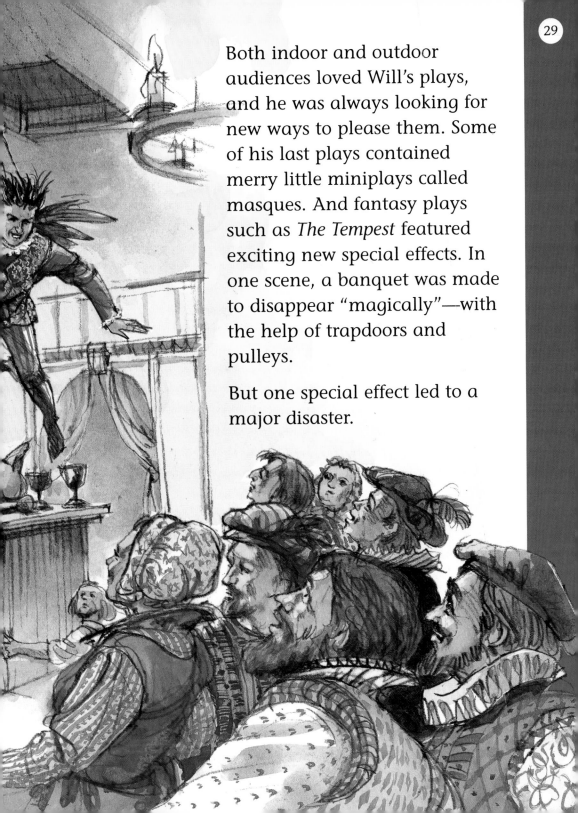

Both indoor and outdoor audiences loved Will's plays, and he was always looking for new ways to please them. Some of his last plays contained merry little miniplays called masques. And fantasy plays such as *The Tempest* featured exciting new special effects. In one scene, a banquet was made to disappear "magically"—with the help of trapdoors and pulleys.

But one special effect led to a major disaster.

As he grew older, Will spent less time in London and more time with his family. He bought more land in Stratford and decided at last to retire there. But he kept in touch with the King's Men, and they still performed his plays. One day in 1613, during a performance of *Henry VIII* at the Globe, a cannon was fired. It set the theater's thatched roof ablaze, and in just two hours the whole building burned to the ground.

Luckily, no one was hurt, and the Globe was soon rebuilt. The written copies of Will's plays were saved, too. In 1623 all 36 plays were put together in a printed book called the First Folio. But Will himself never saw the book. He died in 1616, at the age of 52.

Although he was gone, he would never be forgotten. "My project," said the magician in *The Tempest*, "was to please." Will Shakespeare, the master playwright, still pleases readers and playgoers all over the world today.

Important dates in Shakespeare's life

Index